LEARN, DRAW & COLOR

Animals

ISBN 978-1-64124-308-7

To learn more about the other great books from Fox Chapel Publishing,
or to find a retailer near you, call toll-free 800-457-9112
or visit us at
www.FoxChapelPublishing.com.

We are always looking for talented authors. To submit an idea,
please send a brief inquiry to

acquisitions@foxchapelpublishing.com.

Printed in China
First printing

LEARN, DRAW & COLOR
Animals

**Discover 26 of the
Most Fascinating Animals
on the Planet!**

Happy Fox
BOOKS

Welcome

Discover 26 of the most fascinating animals on the planet!

Learn all about where they live, what makes them so unique, and how they go about their everyday lives. Impress your friends with fun facts—for example, did you know that a flamingo is pink because of the food it eats?!

You'll also learn how to draw each animal in just a few simple steps. Plus, there are 26 full-page pictures for you to color in.

Have fun!

COLORING TOOLS

Using whatever medium you like, bring these delightful animal designs to life! Different coloring tools can create super cool effects and moods to an illustration—for example, markers make more a vibrant statement, while colored pencils are easy to blend and offer a softer feel. Have fun experimenting with some of these mediums:

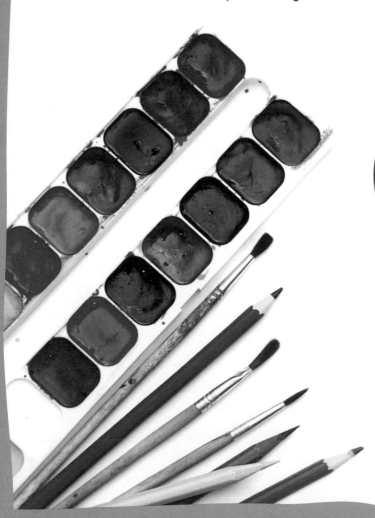

- **Markers**
- **Colored pencils**
- **Colored pens**
- **Gel pens**
- **Watercolors**
- **Crayons**

COLOR THEORY

With color, illustrations take on a life of their own. Remember: when it comes to painting and coloring, there are no rules. The most fun part is to play with color, relax, and enjoy the process and the beautiful, finished result. Feel free to mix and match colors and tones. Work your way from primary colors to secondary colors to tertiary colors, combining different tones to create all kinds of different effects. If you aren't familiar with color theory, here is a quick, easy guide to the basic colors and combinations you will be able to create.

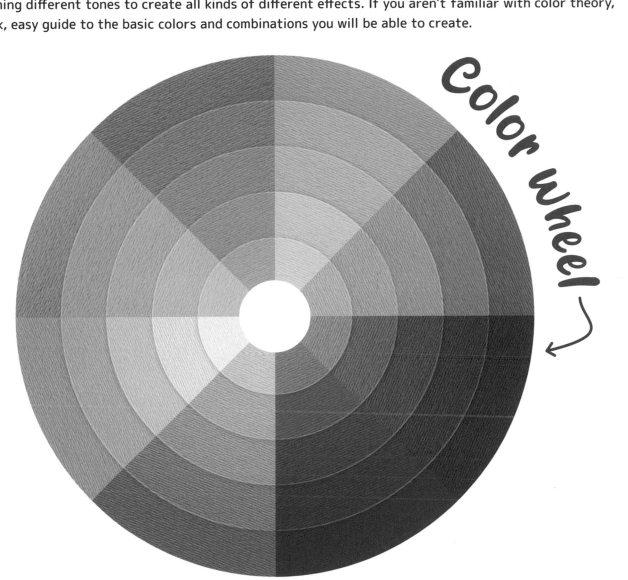

Color wheel

Primary colors:

These are the colors that cannot be obtained by mixing any other colors; they are yellow, blue, and red.

Secondary colors:

These colors are obtained by mixing two primary colors in equal parts; they are green, purple, and orange.

Tertiary colors:

These colors are obtained by mixing one primary color and one secondary color.

Cont

ents

LION

THE KING OF THE JUNGLE—OR IS IT?

The lion is one of the world's most famous animals. From that impressive mane to that fearsome roar, everything about the lion shows its power. These big cats are often called "the king of the jungle," but lions don't actually live in the jungle! They can be found in the African savanna or Asian forest. Lions live in big groups called prides where all members work together to protect and feed each other. Although male lions are bigger than the females, the lionesses are the ones who do most of the hunting. They can chase down and catch prey as big as elephants and giraffes, although a lion's normal diet will be buffalo, antelope, or other smaller mammals.

The lion's golden-brown coat enables it to blend in with its surroundings to help it hunt.

Fun Fact
Centuries ago lions could be found in the Middle East & Europe.

Did you know...
There are around 670 Asian lions in the wild in India. They are smaller than African lions.

©Getty / Henrica Muller

©Getty / Martin Ruegner

Did you know...

Most adult male lions are forced out of their pride. They wander alone until they can take over another pride.

LION
FACT FILE

CLASS
MAMMAL

GROUP NAME
PRIDE

TERRITORY
AFRICAN SAVANNA & INDIAN FOREST

AVERAGE LIFE SPAN
10—15 YEARS

DIET
CARNIVORE
OTHER MAMMALS SUCH AS WARTHOG, ANTELOPE, AND BUFFALO

Male lions start growing their manes from the age of about one.

HOW BIG!

STORM CHASERS

Lions don't only rely on their strength to hunt. They also have brilliant night vision, work as a group to attack their prey from all sides, and sometimes hunt during storms so prey can't hear them coming.

How to draw... a lion

1. HEAD AND MANE: Draw a big circle and create a head shape like this in the middle.

2. MANE AND TAIL: Add lots of lines from the edge of the face out to the circle like this. Draw a long curved line down for the lion's back and tail, plus a flat line for its bottom.

3. FOOT: From the straight line, add a foot and back leg like this.

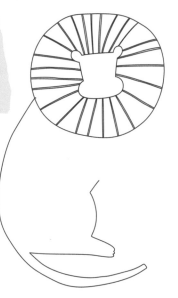

4. FRONT FEET: Starting from the righthand side of the head, draw a line down and add two front legs.

5. FACE: Follow the steps above to create the lion's face.

1. Lines 2. Nose and mouth 3. Eyes and ears

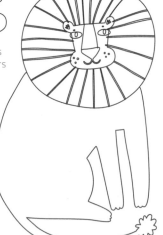

Add a fluffy pom-pom at the end of the tail!

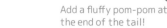

6. COLOR! How about a lovely yellow for its mane, and an orange or brown for its body?

BUTTERFLY

NATURE'S TRANSFORMERS ARE WINGED WONDERS

Butterflies are one of the most instantly recognizable insects in the world, and a common sight in gardens and meadows. They have four beautifully patterned wings, a thin body, and two antennae on top of their head. But they don't always look so magical. Butterflies start out as an egg and hatch into caterpillars. They then wrap themselves up in a silk cocoon, where they completely transform and emerge some time later as an amazing butterfly! They're also really important to the ecosystem because many butterfly species help flowers to reproduce. As they flutter between different flowers to drink nectar (a sugary liquid), they also spread pollen from plant to plant.

©Getty / Paul Souders

Fun Fact

There are about 17,500 different species of butterfly around the world.

?Did you know...

Butterfly wings are actually transparent, or clear! They are covered with tiny scales that reflect the light in amazing colors.

Butterflies lay their eggs on plants so the caterpillars have plenty to eat when they hatch.

The long, slim tube that comes out the middle of a butterfly's head is called a proboscis. They use it like a straw to drink nectar.

MONARCH BUTTERFLY

FACT FILE

- - - - - - - -

CLASS
INSECT

GROUP NAME
FLUTTER

TERRITORY
GLOBAL

HOW SMALL!

AVERAGE LIFE SPAN
6—8 MONTHS

DIET
HERBIVORE
NECTAR

Did you know...

? Some species of butterfly migrate thousands of miles to find warm weather.

OLD TIMERS

Scientists recently discovered that butterflies are much older than we thought. Butterfly remains were found in a fossil that was 200 million years old! This means that butterflies existed before the first birds, flowering plants, and even dinosaurs evolved.

How to draw... a butterfly

1. BODY: Copy this simple outline as your starting point.

2. WINGS: Draw the shape you want the wings to be. To get them symmetrical, make a stencil out of card for one side, then flip it and draw around it for the opposite side.

3. HEAD: Add some long antennae to the top of the head.

4. DECORATE! This is where you can design the pattern on the wings. Remember, butterflies have symmetrical, mirrored markings.

5. DETAILS: We've also added a few small dots and petal shapes, but you can keep it as simple or as detailed as you like!

6. COLOR! Butterflies come in an array of different colors, so go for it! The more colorful, the better.

WHALE

THE WORLD'S BIGGEST BEAST WITH THE SMALLEST DIET

Whales are the largest animals alive today. In fact, the blue whale is the biggest and heaviest animal to have ever lived—even bigger than the dinosaurs! They can grow to an astonishing 100 feet long, and weigh as much as 200 tons. That's the same as about 30 elephants! Even the very smallest whales, like the dwarf sperm whale, are larger than an adult human. Whales are found in every ocean, and can live in both warm and cold waters. Surprisingly, some of the biggest whales feed on very small prey. Most large whales eat krill (tiny crustaceans), which they filter out of the water through their hair-like "teeth." Some whale species, like humpbacks, also hunt for fish.

Fun Fact
Blue whales can eat up to 4 tons of krill every day!

Whales have a thick layer of blubber (fat) around their bodies to keep them warm.

©Getty / Amanda Fletcher

Did you know...
Orcas (or killer whales) are one of the few whales that hunt other mammals, like seals.

The sounds of whales communicating underwater can travel for thousands of miles.

HUMPBACK WHALE

FACT FILE

CLASS
MAMMAL

GROUP NAME
POD

TERRITORY
OCEANS OF THE WORLD

AVERAGE LIFE SPAN
80—90 YEARS

HOW BIG!

DIET
CARNIVORE
KRILL

? Did you know...

Whales can't breathe under water. They come to the surface to breathe through their blowholes.

BREACH FOR THE SKY

When a whale leaps out of the water, it's called breaching. They do this for several reasons: sometimes it's to remove barnacles from their skin, or to help their digestion. Other times, whales can breach as a way of communicating, or just to have fun!

How to draw... a whale

1. BODY: Start by drawing a flat-bottomed pear on its side.

2. FLICK OF THE TAIL: Start to draw the lines upwards from the back of the body. Draw two leaves opposite each other to make the tip of the tail.

3. A BIG SMILE: At the bottom of where the face will be, draw in a big smiley mouth.

You can use an eraser to rub out the original line and create one continuous shape!

4. FIN AND BELLY: In line with the mouth, draw a fin. Then add a tummy underneath.

5. HELLO! Adding an eye, a circle for the cheek, and extra detail to the tail, really brings this whale to life!

6. COLOR! You can add some stripes to the belly, and some barnacle marks for added detail if you want. The finishing details are up to you—make it your own!

PANDA

CHINA'S SYMBOLIC BLACK-AND-WHITE BEAR

High in the mountain forests of China lives one of the world's most famous animals: the giant panda. They are some of the most relaxed creatures on the planet, spending up to 16 hours a day munching on bamboo—their main source of food. Because bamboo doesn't provide much energy, they need to eat lots of it to avoid going hungry. Some pandas eat up to 40% of their body weight in bamboo each day! Pandas were endangered for a while, because their natural habitats are at risk and they find it difficult to breed. However, thanks to conservation efforts, their numbers in the wild are now increasing!

©GettyPansLaos

Fun Fact

Pandas don't roar like other bears. They make bleating sounds. A bit like lambs!

Did you know...

Pandas can hold bamboo thanks to the thumb-like bone that pokes out from their wrist.

Did you know...

Pandas are surprisingly good swimmers and climbers—for an animal that spends most of the day sitting down!

Although pandas mostly eat bamboo, they will sometimes eat fish, eggs, and rodents.

PANDA
FACT FILE

CLASS
MAMMAL

GROUP NAME
EMBARRASSMENT

TERRITORY
FORESTS OF CHINA

HOW BIG!

AVERAGE LIFE SPAN
20 YEARS

DIET
OMNIVORE
MOSTLY BAMBOO, BUT SOMETIMES RODENTS, FISH, AND EGGS

NOT SO GIANT PANDAS

When they are born, baby pandas are just 5 in long, and weigh around 3.5 oz. They are about 900 times smaller than their mothers—which is one of the biggest differences in size between mother and baby of any mammal!

How to draw... a panda

1.HEAD AND BODY: Draw a round shape for the head and a slightly larger oval for the body.

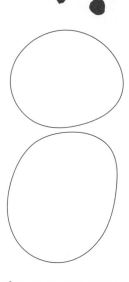

2. ARMS: In between the head and the body, draw in two arms that hug around the top of the body. Color them in black.

3. LEGS: Give your bear some legs. You can keep things simple by drawing them as one continuous shape like this. Color these in black too.

4. PEEK-A-BOO! Draw two small eyes and some black ears on top of the head.

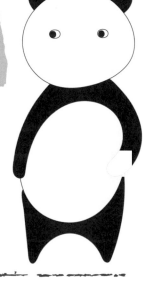

5. PANDA EYES: Color in some black patches around your panda's eyes like this. Then add the nose and mouth.

6. BAMBOO: Finish by giving your panda some tasty bamboo to munch on!

FROG

THIS AMPHIBIAN IS FEELING A BIT JUMPY

Frogs are extraordinary animals that have lots of interesting adaptations and abilities. First of all, they are one of the best jumpers in the animal kingdom. Many species of frog can jump between 20 and 30 times the length of their own bodies. If humans could do the same, then an adult could leap the length of two buses! A female frog lays up to 4,000 eggs in a pond, encased in a kind of jelly. These all clump together to create frogspawn. After a few weeks, these hatch into tadpoles, and then transform into frogs. How weird is that?

© Getty | Oxford Scientific

Fun Fact

The world's biggest frog is the goliath frog—it can grow as big as a cat.

© Getty Bjorn Holland

Frogs don't drink water like we do—they absorb it through their skin instead.

? Did you know...
The most poisonous frog in the world is the golden poison frog. It has enough poison to kill ten adult humans!

Blinking helps frogs to swallow. It squeezes their eyes into their heads, which in turn helps push food down their throat!

RED-EYED TREE FROG

FACT FILE

CLASS
AMPHIBIAN

GROUP NAME
ARMY

TERRITORY
MEXICO, CENTRAL AMERICA & COLOMBIA

HOW SMALL!

AVERAGE LIFE SPAN
5 YEARS

DIET
CARNIVORE
INSECTS

?Did you know...
Frogs and toads are similar, but frogs hop and prefer to be near or in water. Toads crawl and are fine on dry land.

JUMP AROUND

When frogs prepare to jump, they squat and store up energy in their tendons—not their leg muscles. They then burst forward at incredible speeds, which is how they are able to jump so far.

How to draw... a frog

1. TEDDY BEAR: Draw a head in the shape of a teddy bear with big ears. Add circles inside, and color in the pupils like we have here.

2. SMILE! Add a huge smile at the bottom of the head.

3. LEGS: Draw the body as shown, then two loops on either side of the body. This might look odd at this stage, but don't worry—it will work when the feet are added!

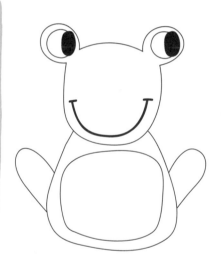

4. FLOWER FEET: At the bottom corners of the body, draw two large feet. Think of petals on a flower for the loops of the toes.

5. STICK OUT YOUR TONGUE: Draw in a long, stretchy tongue hanging down from the mouth. Add the front legs and feet.

You can use an eraser to rub out the original line to create one continuous shape.

6. COLOR! We've added some extra details with dots on the face, legs, and toes. You could even color the eyes red like the red-eyed tree frog!

SLOTH

SLOW AND STEADY WINS THE RACE

The word "sloth" means being slow or lazy, so it's a perfect name for the world's slowest mammal! The sloth moves at an incredibly steady pace. At its average speed, a sloth would take nearly 50 minutes to complete a 100-meter race! They also spend 15 hours a day sleeping. This is because they don't get many calories from their diet of leaves, so they have to save their energy. Sloths spend most of their lives hanging in trees where they are safer from predators. They are a bit clumsy and often fall out of trees! But their bodies are adapted to survive these falls, so they don't usually get hurt.

Sloths really struggle to see in bright conditions. They spend most of their time searching for shade.

©Getty Vanhaug Grubleset

Did you know...
Baby sloths are able to cling on to their mother's fur as soon as they are born.

Sloths eat leaves and twigs, but it can take them up to a month to digest a single leaf!

PALE-THROATED SLOTH

FACT FILE

CLASS
MAMMAL

GROUP NAME
SNUGGLE

TERRITORY
SOUTH AMERICAN
RAINFOREST

HOW BIG!

AVERAGE LIFE SPAN
20—30 YEARS

DIET
HERBIVORE
LEAVES AND TWIGS

Fun Fact

Sloths are surprisingly good swimmers and can actually swim three times faster than their walking speed.

Did you know...

A sloth's internal organs are able to keep working normally even when it is hanging upside down.

COMING DOWN TO EARTH

Sloths only come out of their trees for three reasons: one is to find food, another is to find a mate, and the third is to go to the bathroom! They only poo once a week and can get rid of a third of their body weight when they go!

How to draw... a sloth

1. TO START: Draw a nice big branch for your sloth to call home.

2. SWINGING HAPPY: Start drawing the body shape as shown.. You will need to erase some of the branch lines to make it look like the back foot is in front of the tree.

3. HEAD: Start with the outline of the head as shown here, adding some fluffy hair. Draw a slightly smaller fluffy shape inside. In the middle of that, add an oval for the snout.

4. FACE AND TUMMY: Add a nose and mouth inside the snout. Then draw in some cute eyes and cheeks on either side of the snout. Draw a teardrop-shaped tummy.

5. A GOOD GRIP: Draw in the last back leg so it goes behind the branch. Then add some big claws to help it hold on!

6. COLOR! Make sure you give your sloth its distinctive dark eye markings! Add some texture to the fur by using a darker brown marker and make lots of dashes.

30

PENGUIN

THE FLIGHTLESS BIRD THAT'S A WHIZZ IN THE WATER

When most people imagine a bird, they'll think of a soaring eagle, swooping owl, or fluttering robin. But some birds can't fly! Penguins are flightless birds, and their wings are better suited to swimming than flying. Their small, flat wings are more like flippers, making penguins speedy swimmers as they search for fish to eat. Nearly all penguins live in the coldest parts of the Southern hemisphere—around Antarctica, and the southern tips of Africa, Australia, and South America. They can survive extremely cold and windy conditions thanks to their thick coats of fluffy feathers. Their outer feathers are also waterproof to keep them dry. Some penguins even huddle together in groups to keep each other warm!

Fun Fact
Emperor penguins are considered the giants of the penguin world.

©Getty / VMJones

Did you know...
The fastest penguins are gentoo penguins. They can swim at speeds of up to 22 mph!

Penguins are able to safely drink seawater because their bodies can filter out the salt. They then sneeze the salt out!

Emperor penguins have lots of short, extra fluffy feathers close to their skin to help keep them warm. They can survive freezing temperatures as low as -58°F!

EMPEROR PENGUIN

FACT FILE

CLASS
BIRD

GROUP NAME
WADDLE

TERRITORY
ANTARCTICA

HOW BIG!

AVERAGE LIFE SPAN
15—20 YEARS

DIET
CARNIVORE
FISH

? Did you know...
Penguins' black backs and white bellies are good camouflage in the water. It is tricky for predators to spot them from above or below.

BABY CARE

After the female penguin lays an egg, the male penguin takes care of it until it hatches. The female swims off for several weeks to find food. When she comes back, she feeds the chicks by bringing partly digested food back up to her throat. Gross!

33

How to draw... a penguin

1. SIMPLE SHAPE: Is it a tall rainbow? A hill? A door? No, it's the start of your penguin's body!

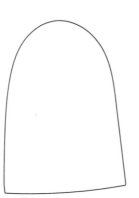

2. REPEAT: Inside the body shape, draw a smaller arch.

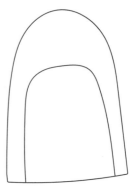

3. WOBBLY FEET: To make the penguin look like it's waddling along, draw one foot slightly higher than the other.

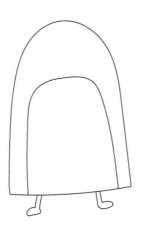

4. EYES AND BEAK: Just above the tummy, draw two eyes and a small triangle for the beak in the middle.

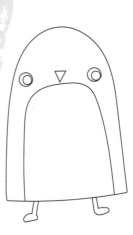

5. FLIPPERS: Draw a flipper on each side of the body, just below the eyes. Erase the original lines on the sides so the flippers become part of the body.

6. COLOR! You can make your penguin very colorful if you like! Or stick with the classic black and white, with orange or red for the beak and feet.

CHAMELEON

THERE'S MORE TO THIS COLORFUL CHARACTER THAN MEETS THE (WEIRD) EYE!

The chameleon is one of the most fascinating animals in the world. Its most famous feature is the ability to change color. People used to think this was for camouflage, but chameleons actually change color depending on their mood and temperature. Dark and dull colors show that it's cold or stressed, while brighter colors show it's warm or relaxed. Chameleons' eyes are also pretty amazing. Each eye can move independently, giving these reptiles incredible 360-degree vision. The way they catch their prey is awesome too. They flick out their long, sticky tongue at 60 miles per hour to catch passing insects. Imagine if humans could do that!

Fun Fact
There are more than 200 chameleon species. Most of them live in Africa.

©Getty / Mike Powles

Chameleons use their long tail to wrap around trees and branches while climbing.

Did you know...
The Brookesia group of chameleons includes some of the world's smallest reptiles.

PANTHER CHAMELEON

FACT FILE
- - - - - -

CLASS
REPTILE

GROUP NAME
CAMOUFLAGE

TERRITORY
MADAGASCAR

AVERAGE LIFE SPAN
1—5 YEARS

DIET
OMNIVORE
INSECTS AND LEAVES

HOW SMALL!

No nearby insect is safe from a chameleon's long, sticky and super quick tongue. Watch out!

? Did you know...
A chameleon's tongue is usually twice the length of its body. It's also sticky to help catch prey.

COLOR CODING
How do chameleons perform their party trick? It's all thanks to special cells in their skin that reflect light in different ways to produce different colors. Chameleons can change the sizes of these cells, which in turn changes the color they appear.

How to draw... a chameleon

1. HEAD: Start by drawing the head shape, like this.

2. BODY: Next, draw two curved lines from the head to create the body.

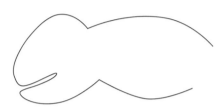

3. TWIRLY TAIL: For the amazing curly tail, start from the top end of the body at the back, and draw a big swirl. Then follow the line back up, but leave a bit of space in between so it joins the bottom of the body. Add a branch just below the body.

4. SCALES AND CLAWS! Add spiky scales all the way down the back, and a few under the chin. Then draw in two feet so your chameleon is standing on the branch, and give it some claws.

5. NOW THAT'S A TONGUE! Just like the tail, create a long, curly tongue. Finally, add some big, googly eyes.

Don't forget, you can tidy up any lines with an eraser once you have finished!

6. MASTERS OF COLOR: What color will you make your chameleon? These reptiles have the amazing ability to change their color. . . so be quick before it changes its mind!

RACCOON

THE CUTE MASKED RAIDER THAT HAS STOLEN MANY HEARTS

The raccoon is a cat-sized mammal that can mostly be found in North and South America. It has a dark band of fur around its eyes, which looks like the mask of a superhero or a bandit! Raccoons are nocturnal, which means they are mostly active at night. They naturally live in forests, but it's common to see them roaming in towns and cities. These urban raccoons can often be spotted rummaging around in people's bins looking for leftover food—they're certainly not picky eaters! Out in the wild, they'll eat fish, eggs, and small mammals, as well as nuts and berries. Raccoons are very clever and they are especially good at problem solving. They can figure out how to undo locks and open windows!

Fun Fact

Raccoons don't hibernate, but they can spend most of the winter asleep to save energy when food is harder to find.

Raccoons are strong climbers, and sleep in tree hollows.

©Getty / Wolfgang Kaehler

Did you know...

It's a myth that raccoons "wash" their food. But wet paws can improve their sense of touch.

Scientists think that raccoons can recognize each other by their unique mask patterns.

NORTHERN RACCOON,

FACT FILE

CLASS
MAMMAL

GROUP NAME
GAZE

TERRITORY
NORTH AMERICAN FOREST

HOW SMALL!

AVERAGE LIFE SPAN
2—3 YEARS

DIET
OMNIVORE
FISH, SMALL MAMMALS, FRUIT, NUTS, SEEDS

? Did you know...

Raccoons are pretty quick critters! They can run at speeds of up to 15 mph!

SUPER SENSITIVE

Raccoon paws are incredibly sensitive. They have lots of special nerve cells in their front paws (more than we have in our hands) so they have an excellent sense of touch. Before eating, raccoons will pick up and hold their food to figure out what it is.

How to draw... a raccoon

1. MUSHROOM:
Start with an oval "eye" shape for the head. Then add the body shape underneath, which will make it look a bit like a mushroom!

2. EARS AND TUMMY:
Inside the body, draw curved lines from the head to the top of the legs. Then add the ears at the top of the head.

3. ARMS AND TAIL:
Inside the tummy line, draw in two arms. Add a bushy tail on its lefthand side.

4. FACE:
Draw a curved "m" shape on the top half of the head. Add a nose On the middle point. Add two wide stripes on either side.

1. Forehead and nose

2. Cheek stripes

5. EYES AND MOUTH:
Draw two cute eyes inside the stripes, and finish with a mischevious smile under the nose.

6. COLOR!
You could use different shades of gray and black, as shown here, or get creative and make a rainbow raccoon! Don't forget to make the tail stripy!

43

CRAB

THESE CRUSTACEANS ARE FAR FROM CRUSTY AND BORING!

Crabs are a kind of crustacean, like shrimp, lobster and krill. Most of them have a tough outer shell called an exoskeleton, like a natural Iron Man suit! Crabs have ten legs, but two of these are claws called pincers. These are used to catch prey and for fighting other crabs. Some crabs have incredibly powerful pincers that are strong enough to crack open coconuts—you certainly don't want a crab to grab your finger! Crabs are famous for walking sideways instead of forwards. This is because their leg joints bend at the side, so it's easier to walk in that direction. Try walking sideways and you'll see how tricky it would be for a crab to walk forwards!

©Getty / Lesopisang

Crabs generally use one pincer to hold on to food and the other to put bits of it into their mouths.

©Getty / Khaichuin Sim

? Did you know...
Crabs that live in water breathe through gills like fish, but land crabs have lungs.

Crabs can be found in marine environments pretty much everywhere in the world.

Fun Fact

Hermit crabs don't have hard shells to protect themselves. Instead, they find empty shells to wear as armor!

RED ROCK CRAB

FACT FILE

CLASS
MALACOSTRACA
A TYPE OF CRUSTACEAN

GROUP NAME
CAST

TERRITORY
WESTERN COAST OF SOUTH AMERICA

HOW SMALL!

AVERAGE LIFE SPAN
5 YEARS

DIET
OMNIVORE
SPONGES, MOLLUSCS, OTHER CRABS, EGGS

Did you know...

Male fiddler crabs have one claw that's much larger than the other. It's used for fighting and attracting a mate.

MOVING HOME

Crabs are invertebrates, which means they don't have a backbone. They're covered in a hard shell that protects them from predators, but it isn't very flexible. As they grow, the shell splits and they wriggle out. They then grow a new shell within a few days.

How to draw... a crab

1. BODY: Start by drawing a big oval.

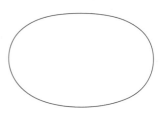

2. EIGHT LEGS: Along the bottom of the oval, draw four pointy legs on the left, and four on the right.

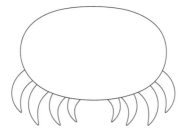

3. ARMS: Draw two arms that curve upwards. Add rounded triangles to the ends like this.

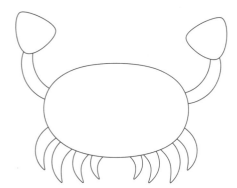

4. PINCERS: Add the all-important pincers on top of the arms. Make sure the outside claws are bigger. At the very top of the body, draw two eye stalks.

5. LASHINGS OF LASHES: Add eyes to the tops of the stalks, and add some eyelashes. This crab isn't crabby, so add a nice smile too!

6. CRABULOUS! Crabs come in all different colors, so go for it! The world's your oyster (or crab!).

ELEPHANT

THE GENTLE GIANTS THAT ARE UNDER THREAT

Elephants are the largest land animals on the planet. They grow up to 13 feet tall and can weigh over seven tons—about the same as five family cars! There are three species of elephant that live in different regions: Asian elephants, African savanna elephants, and African forest elephants. The two African species are larger than their Asian cousins, but all elephants are pretty hefty! Sadly, these gentle giants are under threat, and their numbers in the wild are decreasing. Illegal hunters target elephants for their ivory tusks. There are now about 450,000 left in the wild. Elephants are intelligent, beautiful creatures that must be protected for future generations to love.

Fun Fact
Elephants throw mud and sand over themselves to protect against the hot sun—just like a sunscreen!

©Getty / kizsonpascal

Did you know...
In one day, adult elephants can eat up to 330 lb of grass, fruit, and bark!

African elephants are a keystone species. This means that the impact they have on the environment helps other animals thrive.

An elephant's trunk contains more than 40,000 muscles. They are used for gathering food, drinking, breathing, and trumpeting.

AFRICAN SAVANNA ELEPHANT

FACT FILE

CLASS
MAMMAL

GROUP NAME
HERD

TERRITORY
AFRICAN PLAINS

AVERAGE LIFE SPAN
60—70 YEARS

DIET
HERBIVORE
PLANTS AND FRUIT

CONSERVATION STATUS
ENDANGERED

HOW BIG!

Did you know...

? Elephant pregnancies last for 22 months. It's the longest pregnancy of any mammal!

AFRICAN VS ASIAN

Size isn't the only difference between African and Asian elephants. African elephants have larger ears than Asian elephants. Amazingly, Asian elephant ears are shaped a bit like Asia, while African elephants have Africa-shaped ears!

How to draw...
an elephant

1. HEAD AND TRUNK: Draw a balloon shape, and then add a trunk shape on the righthand side like this.

Add the trunk shape and then erase the line here.

2. BODY: Starting from the back of the head, draw a sloped line that gently curves down to create the back leg. Draw an arch shape to add the front leg.

3. LEGS AND TOES: Draw in the other two legs behind the ones you've just drawn. Then add toenails to all of the feet.

4. EARS: Draw a big "C" shape with a smaller one inside to create the ear on the left. Do the same but flipped for the right ear.

5. FACE AND TAIL: Draw a little tail at the back, then add eyes, a cheek, and a mouth. Create some wrinkle lines along the trunk.

Erase the body line that's going through the ear.

6. COLOR! Why not add some tufts of hair on the top of the head, and maybe a squirt of water coming out of the trunk?

TOUCAN

THIS COLORFUL BIRD REALLY FITS THE BILL

While a very large bill at a restaurant might be a bad thing, the very large bill on a toucan is a brilliant thing! Toucans live in the tropical forests of South America, and they are famous for their huge, brightly colored bills. These birds use their big bills to reach and peel tropical fruit to eat. Although fruit makes up most of a toucan's diet, they will also eat insects and small reptiles. Scientists discovered that toucans' bills help to control their body temperature, like a personal radiator! It is also thought that a bigger and brighter bill helps male toucans to attract a mate.

A toucan's bill is surprisingly good camouflage among the bright colors of tropical plants.

Fun Fact

Toucans aren't very good at flying! They prefer to hop around the forest instead!

© Getty / JaimSimoesOliveira

Did you know...

Baby toucans' bills are much smaller compared to their bodies, but they grow rapidly.

Toucans nest in tree hollows. They often move into hollows that have already been made by other birds, like woodpeckers.

TOCO TOUCAN

FACT FILE

CLASS
BIRD

GROUP NAME
DURANTE

TERRITORY
SOUTH AMERICAN TROPICAL FOREST

HOW BIG!

AVERAGE LIFE SPAN
20 YEARS

DIET
OMNIVORE
FRUIT, EGGS, REPTILES

? Did you know...

Toucans use their bills to help control their body temperature. They can tuck it under their wings to stay warm at night.

LIGHT AND AIRY

A toucan's bill might be big, but it's actually very light. It's mostly made of keratin, which is the same protein that makes up human fingernails and rhino horns. It also has a structure like honeycomb, so there are lots of air gaps inside to make it lighter.

How to draw... a toucan

1. BODY: It might take a bit of practice to get this shape right. You can always draw a long oval for the body instead.

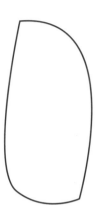

2. WHAT A BEAK! The toucan's beak is huge! Make it as big as the body for this drawing.

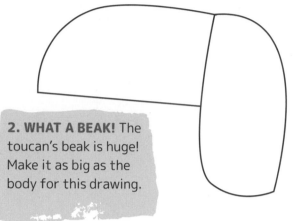

3. MORE DETAIL: Draw a semicircle at the end of the beak. Give your bird a big smile, and add two big circles to the top of the body.

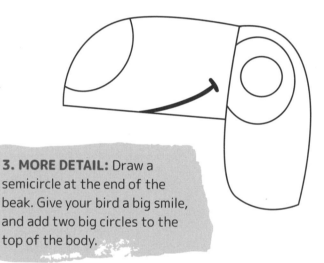

4. WINGS AND FEET! Draw two wings on the body, then add some thin legs and walking feet.

5. EYE AND TAIL: Draw a big eye in the middle circle. Finally, add a triangle at the bottom of the toucan for its tail, with some lines to create feathers.

6. COLOR, COLOR AND MORE COLOR! Do this colorful bird justice—bright and bold is the way to go!

KOALA

THE "BEAR" THAT'S DEFINITELY NOT A BEAR!

Koalas are cute and fluffy mammals that live in the trees of Australia. They are sometimes known as "koala bears," but they're not bears at all! Koalas are actually marsupials, like kangaroos. Marsupials carry their young in a special pouch on their bellies until the babies are old enough to eat their own food. Koalas have a diet of eucalyptus leaves, which they chomp on for around three hours every day. They then spend up to 20 hours sleeping and digesting their dinner—what an easy life! Koalas rarely come down from their trees, as they're pretty slow at moving across the ground. They spend most of their lives eating, sleeping, and raising their young high up away from predators.

©Getty / Arun Roisri

There are more than 700 species of eucalyptus tree, but koalas only like the leaves of about 50. Fussy eaters!

Fun Fact

Despite rarely coming down from the trees, koalas are pretty good swimmers!

©Getty / Zerin Unal / EyeEm

? Did you know...

Eucalyptus leaves are toxic to most animals, but koalas can digest them easily.

These cuddly creatures need lots of space. Their ideal habitat will have at least 100 trees per koala!

KOALA
FACT FILE

CLASS
MAMMAL

GROUP NAME
CLING

TERRITORY
AUSTRALIAN FORESTS

HOW BIG!

AVERAGE LIFE SPAN
10—15 YEARS

DIET
HERBIVORE
EUCALYPTUS LEAVES

? Did you know...

Koalas have very supportive bottoms that keep them comfy while they sit on branches all day.

POUCH POTATOES

Baby koalas are called joeys and crawl straight into their mother's pouches after being born. They stay there for five to seven months, then once they get too big for the pouch they are carried on the mother's back until they're about one year old.

How to draw... a koala

1. HEAD: Think of a slightly square circle when you are drawing the head. Add a tiny tuft of fur at the top.

2. EARS: On either side of the head, near the top, draw its ears. Start with the outside shape, and then draw the same shape but smaller inside each ear.

3. BACK AND TAIL: Start underneath the chin on the left side. Draw a curved line down and round to create a back foot. Add a fluffy tail at the back too.

4. FRONT LEG: Start underneath the chin on the right side. Draw a front leg like this. Add a fluffy furry chest.

5. SLEEPY FACE: Draw a big nose in the lower half of the koala's face. Then on either side, draw two "u" shapes for the sleepy eyes. Add some little eyebrows and a small mouth.

6. COLOR! Scribble on some pink cheeks for a cute look! Don't forget to give your koala some tasty leaves to eat as well.

SNAKE

THESE SLITHERING SERPENTS ARE SERIOUSLY SUPER PREDATORS

Snakes certainly look a little bit scary, but they don't really deserve their reputation. Most snakes have long, slithery bodies that are covered in scales, tiny black eyes, and a long, forked tongue. There are nearly 4,000 species of snake and they're found all over the world. But most of them are harmless to humans! These reptiles catch their prey in different ways. Some will paralyze their prey with venom from a bite. Bigger snakes, like the boa constrictor, wrap around their prey and crush it. Other species simply catch their prey and swallow it while it's still alive! Most snakes will try their best to avoid humans, and won't attack unless they are scared or hurt.

Did you know...
Snakes regularly shed their skin as they grow, or as it gets worn out. This is called molting.

Fun Fact
Snakes can be found on every continent in the world except Antarctica!

Did you know...
Sea snakes live in the Pacific and Indian Oceans. They don't have gills and must swim to the surface to breathe.

©Getty / Mark Kostich

©Getty / James RD Scott

BALL PYTHON

FACT FILE

CLASS
REPTILE

GROUP NAME
NEST

TERRITORY
WESTERN AND CENTRAL AFRICAN FORESTS AND SAVANNA

HOW BIG!

AVERAGE LIFE SPAN
10 YEARS

DIET
CARNIVORE
SMALL MAMMALS AND BIRDS

Snakes make dens in shaded locations, but they don't make nests for their young.

Some snakes have holes in their faces that sense heat given off by prey.

CHEW YOUR FOOD

Snakes don't use their teeth to chew. Instead, their teeth are used to hold food in place while they swallow food whole. They can unhinge their jaws to eat prey much bigger than themselves. Some snakes have even been seen swallowing down crocodiles and cows!

How to draw... a snake

1. BODY: Start with a flattened circle like this. Then draw two more underneath the first one.

2. TAIL: Add a long, wiggly tail like this.

3. NECK: On the top circle of the body, draw a smaller oval. This is going to be the inside of the coil. Draw a long neck coming up from it.

4. HEAD: On the end of the neck, draw a head, a mouth, and two small eyes.

5. DETAILS: Add nostrils and a long, forked tongue. Then draw on a pattern if you like. We have used spots but you might want a stripy snake instead!

6. COLOR! Snakes come in all sorts of colors and patterns. You can make your snake camouflaged, or cover it in bright colors to stand out!

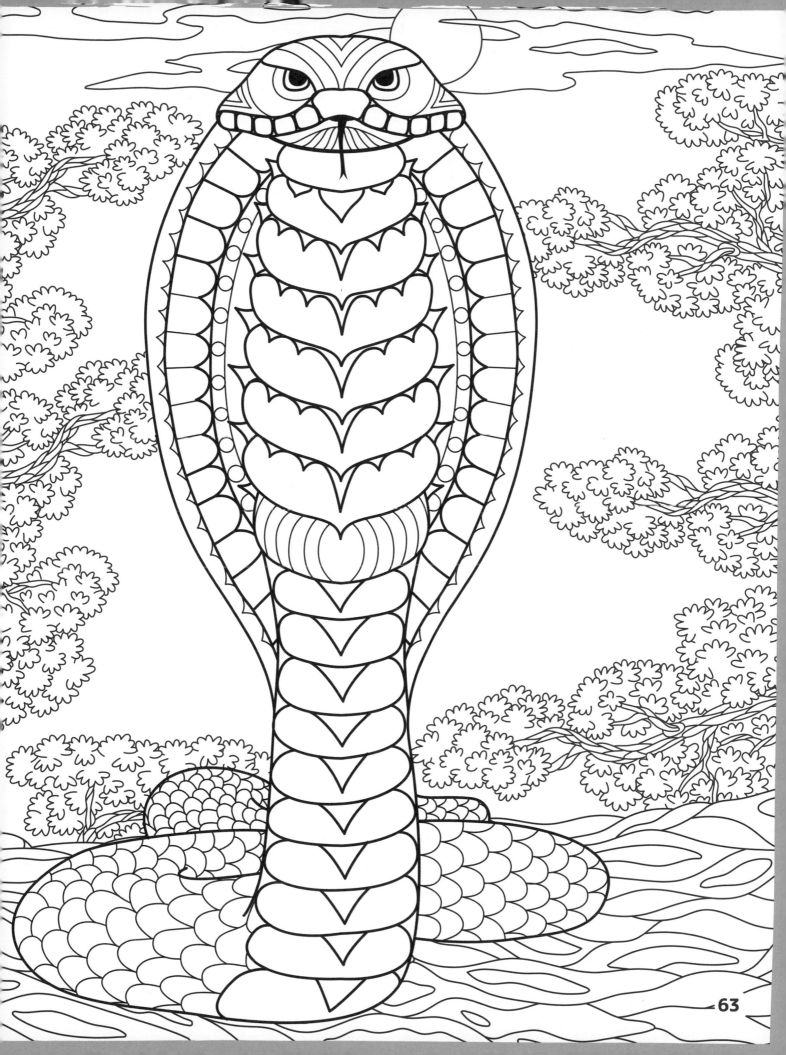

GIRAFFE

THE MOST GRACEFUL GIANT IN ITS NECK OF THE WOODS

The pattern of a giraffe's brown spots are unique, like snowflakes or your fingerprints.

The giraffe is the tallest land animal in the world, measuring between 13 and 20 feet from hoof to head. A lot of that impressive height is made up of its extremely long neck. Giraffes make the most of this unique feature by chomping on leaves from the tallest trees. They have no competition for food because other grazing animals simply can't reach! Giraffes only need to drink once every few days because the leaves they eat contain lots of water. When they do drink, giraffes splay their legs out really wide or kneel down to reach the water. This helps stop blood rushing to their heads!

©Getty / Frieder

? Did you know...

A giraffe's tongue is 18 in long to help it grab the tastiest leaves. It's also a dark purple color!

No other animal on the ground can challenge a giraffe for this tasty meal!

GIRAFFE
FACT FILE

CLASS
MAMMAL

GROUP NAME
TOWER

TERRITORY
AFRICAN SAVANNA

AVERAGE LIFE SPAN
25 YEARS

DIET
HERBIVORE
LEAVES

HOW BIG!

Fun Fact
A baby giraffe can stand up within an hour of being born!

Did you know...
Although they have spindly legs, giraffes aren't slow. They can run at speeds of up to 35 mph!

HEART TO HEART
To get blood pumping all the way up to the top of that long neck, giraffes need a very big heart. The average giraffe heart measures 24 in across, and weighs 25 lbs. In comparison, your heart is roughly the size of your clenched fist!

65

How to draw... a giraffe

1. HEAD: Follow these mini steps to complete the head and face.

1. Outline this shape to start the face.

2. Add a rough circle that overlaps at the bottom.

3. Draw two leaf-shaped ears, then use an eraser to tidy things up by removing the lines that overlap.

4. Add the eyes, the inside of the ears, and the all-important horns (which are called ossicones).

2. LONG NECK: What is a giraffe without an incredibly long neck? Start below the eye on the right and draw straight down. Do the same for the other side, but this time start under the nose.

NECK

Curve the lines out to create the body

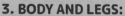

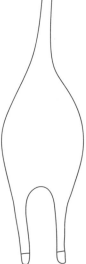

3. BODY AND LEGS: From your neck lines, curve out on each side, and then slope them back in at the bottom. Draw an arch in the middle for the legs, and add lines across for the feet.

4. COLOR! When you are coloring in your giraffe, don't forget the pattern of dark patches on its fur!

OCTOPUS

EIGHT ARMS, THREE HEARTS AND NO BONES!

Octopuses are famous for having eight arms, but that's not the only strange thing about them. They have three hearts: one sends blood around their body, like humans, and the other two send blood to their gills to help them breathe. Octopuses also have nine brains! There is a donut-shaped brain in their head, plus one "mini brain" in each arm to help control their movement. Scientists have put octopus intelligence to the test and found that they can solve puzzles and get out of mazes. They can squeeze through tiny gaps too, which makes them great escape artists. Some aquarium octopuses have even been known to sneak out of their tanks!

©Getty / A. Mar

©Getty / Stuart Westmorland

Fun Fact
The octopus got its name because "octo" means eight in Greek, and "pous" means foot.

Octopuses mostly eat crustaceans or molluscs found on the ocean floor.

Did you know...
Some octopuses can squirt ink for self-defense. It confuses predators while the octopus escapes!

? Did you know...
Octopus's sucker-covered limbs are called arms, not tentacles. Squid and cuttlefish have tentacles, but octopuses don't!

Although octopuses can swim, it makes them tired so they prefer to walk.

BLUE-RINGED OCTOPUS,
FACT FILE

CLASS
CEPHALOPOD

GROUP NAME
TANGLE

TERRITORY
PACIFIC OCEAN

AVERAGE LIFE SPAN
2 YEARS

DIET
CARNIVORE
SMALL CRUSTACEANS AND FISH

HOW SMALL!

BLUE BLOOD
Octopus blood contains copper, which makes it blue! The copper helps to carry oxygen around the octopus's body even in chilly underwater environments. It's not just octopuses either—many crustaceans and molluscs have blue blood too.

How to draw... an octopus

1. HEAD: Follow the mini steps below to create the head.

1. Start with a balloon shape.

2. Draw semicircles on the ends.

3. Add in the eyes.

2. ARMS: Starting under the eye, draw a long, curly line. Once you get to the tip, follow the same shape as you draw the line back up towards the head to make the first arm.

3. HOW MANY? Repeat this process until you have eight wriggly arms.

4. INSIDE LEG: Once you have finished drawing all the arms, add these lines to each one.

5. SUCKERS! Add lots of little circles on the arms for all of the suckers.

6. COLOR CHANGER! Octopuses are incredible! They can change color to blend in with their surroundings. So get creative with your color choices!

Octopuses can change their color, and even the texture of their skin!

LLAMA

MEET THE CAMEL'S FLUFFY SOUTH AMERICAN COUSIN

Llamas are members of the camel family and live in the Andes, a mountain range that runs through South America. They are domesticated animals, meaning they are kept by humans instead of living in the wild. Humans have kept llamas for thousands of years, mainly for their wool and strength. Llamas are really good at carrying things! They can carry over 50 pounds in weight, and travel up to 20 miles in a day. But if they are given too much to carry, they will make a big fuss—and quite right too! They will refuse to move, and might even start spitting or kicking until their owner lightens the load.

Fun Fact
Some farmers use guard llamas to protect their sheep and other animals from predators!

Llamas can cope with rocky, uneven ground because their padded, two-toed feet give them lots of grip.

Did you know...
Llamas communicate using some weird noises, like humming, gargling, and even clucking!

A llama's fleece is thick and tough. It's not terribly comfy, but it's really good at keeping the cold out.

LLAMA
FACT FILE

CLASS
MAMMAL

GROUP NAME
HERD

TERRITORY
ANDES MOUNTAINS OF SOUTH AMERICA

HOW BIG!

AVERAGE LIFE SPAN
20 YEARS

DIET
HERBIVORE GRASS

?

Did you know...

You can tell llamas apart from alpacas because they're taller and have longer faces and bigger ears.

A LOT OF LAMOIDS

Llamas are distantly related to the camels found in the deserts of Africa, Asia, and Australia, but they're part of a separate group called the Lamoids. This is made up of llamas, alpacas, vicuñas, and guanacos. Lamoids don't have humps like their camel cousins do.

73

How to draw... a llama

1. CLOUD BODY: Draw a nice, fluffy cloud! This will be the llama's body.

At the top left, create a bigger curve (this is going to be the tail!).

2. NECK AND HEAD: Next, draw a neck and head shape.

You can erase the original line so it becomes one whole shape.

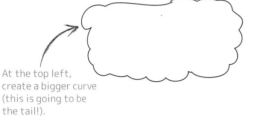

3. EARS: Add some curvy ears.

4. LEGS AND FEET: Next, draw four straight legs with little feet on the end.

1. Draw an egg shape.

2. Add a cute nose.

3. Draw two "u" shapes for the eyes, and add a few eyelashes.

5. FACE: Follow the mini steps above to create the llama's face in the middle of its head.

6. COLOR! Why not design a lovely blanket to go on the back of your llama? In South America, where llamas live, these traditional blankets are usually brightly colored and have detailed patterns.

CROCODILE

READ ALL ABOUT THE CROCODILE – AND MAKE IT SNAPPY!

With their long, powerful bodies, sharp teeth, and eyes that peek out of the water, crocodiles are one of the scariest members of the animal kingdom. But they are also one of the most interesting! Crocodiles have existed for more than 200 million years. They lived at the same time as the dinosaurs, and haven't actually changed much since then, so they must be doing something right! The smallest species is the dwarf crocodile, which is less than 6.5 feet long. Saltwater crocodiles are the biggest, and can grow up to 20 feet long! Crocs usually take their prey by surprise. They'll quietly lurk in the water before lunging very quickly to attack their next meal.

Fun Fact

Crocs are not fussy eaters! They will eat almost anything and sometimes even attack other predators including sharks and big cats!

©Getty/Huda Riger / EyeEm

? Did you know...

Crocodiles cannot chew. They use their powerful jaws to crush prey then swallow it whole or in big chunks.

SALTWATER CROCODILE

FACT FILE

CLASS
REPTILE

GROUP NAME
BASK (ON LAND) FLOAT (IN WATER)

TERRITORY
EASTERN INDIA, SOUTHEAST ASIA & NORTHERN AUSTRALIA

AVERAGE LIFE SPAN
70 YEARS

DIET
CARNIVORE
FISH, MAMMALS, BIRDS, REPTILES, CRUSTACEANS

HOW BIG!

?Did you know...
Crocodiles have a similar life expectancy to humans, but some individuals are thought to be over 100!

The scales at the side of the croc's mouth have pressure sensors in them. These help it to detect movement in the water so it can find prey and plan its attack!

CROC OR GATOR
Crocodiles and alligators look similar, but there are ways to tell them apart. A croc's snout is more V-shaped, and some of its lower teeth are visible when its mouth is shut. An alligator's snout is more U-shaped, and its bottom teeth are hidden.

How to draw... a crocodile

1. BODY: Copy this simple outline as your starting point.

2. NOSTRILS AND EYES: Draw two smaller bobbles at the top of its nose, and then two bigger circles at the top of its head.

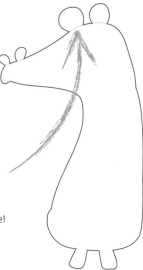

You can use an eraser to rub out the original line and create one continuous shape!

3. WHAT YOU LOOKING AT? Draw a circle inside each of the eyes, and then color in the pupils. Add extra circles inside the nose, then draw a wiggly mouth and a big tummy!

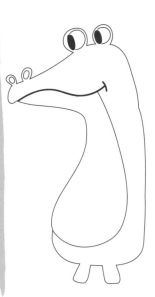

4. THE SHARP PARTS! Add the all-important teeth, then draw some scales down the crocodile's back.

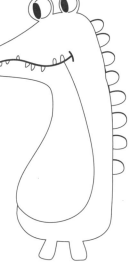

5. LEGS AND TAIL: Draw a tail at the bottom of the body, and two small front legs above the tummy. Add some claws to all four feet.

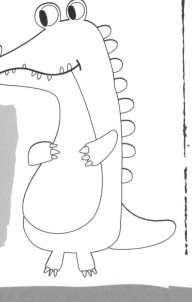

6. COLOR! You can add some stripes to the croc's tummy and tail. We've also given it some freckles and rosy cheeks!

78

HUMMINGBIRD

THIS BRIGHTLY COLORED BIRD IS TINY BUT MIGHTY

Big isn't always better, and that's certainly true when it comes to the hummingbird. These tiny, brightly colored birds can be found across North and South America. They rarely grow any bigger than a human hand, but they are spectacularly speedy. Hummingbirds can fly at speeds of over 30 miles per hour! Not only can they swoop forwards and side to side like normal birds, but they can hover and fly straight down, straight up, and even backwards! This is particularly useful when sipping nectar from plants, as they don't have to worry about landing. They can just fly down, hover while having their dinner, then fly backwards to get their bill out of the plant. Incredible!

Hummingbirds migrate to find good weather. Some travel nearly 4,000 miles!

©Getty / Roberto Machado Noa

? Did you know...
At just 2 in long, the bee hummingbird is the smallest species of bird in the world!

Hummingbirds eat sugary nectar. They can eat half their body weight of it each day.

ANNA'S HUMMINGBIRD

FACT FILE

CLASS
BIRD

GROUP NAME
CHARM

TERRITORY
NORTH AMERICA

AVERAGE LIFE SPAN
8 YEARS

DIET
HERBIVORE
NECTAR

HOW SMALL!

Fun Fact
Some hummingbirds' hearts beat at more than 1,200 beats per minute!

Did you know...
Male hummingbirds show off by diving through the sky really fast. They do this to impress females!

HUM THAT TUNE
Hummingbirds get their name from the sound they make while they fly. Because they flap their wings so incredibly fast (up to around 80 times a second), the vibrations make a humming noise. They also beat their wings in a figure eight shape.

1. BODY: Draw an oval at an angle.

2. HEAD AND TAIL: At the top, draw a head and beak. Then draw a tail at the bottom of the body.

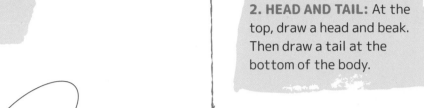

3. EYE AND FEET: Draw a big eye onto the head, then add two little feet.

Tidy up by erasing the lines here.

4. WINGS: Draw two wings, one behind the body, and one in front. Add an extra tail feather here too.

5. BIGGER WINGS: Create a pair of larger wings behind the original ones you created in step 4.

6. COLOR! Hummingbirds are such colorful birds. Go for bright and eye-catching colors. You could also draw a tasty flower for your bird to snack on!

83

MANDRILL

MEET THE WORLD'S BIGGEST AND BRIGHTEST MONKEY

Mandrills are the biggest monkeys in the world. They are also incredibly colorful, with bright red and blue faces (and bottoms!). Mandrills' colored markings actually get even brighter when they are excited or angry. The males are especially colorful because it makes them more attractive to females. These monkeys usually live in groups of about 20 females and their young, led by one adult male. Sometimes, lots of different mandrill groups join together in much larger crowds called hordes. The biggest hordes can include more than 1,000 mandrills! They spend most of their time on the ground looking for food, but will climb up into the safety of the trees when they need to sleep.

Fun Fact

Mandrills choose a different tree to sleep in every single evening!

You might recognize this monkey from the Disney film *The Lion King*—the character Rafiki is a mandrill!

©Getty/Thomas Kitchin & Victoria Hurst / Design Pics

Did you know...

Mandrills might look scary when they show their long, pointy teeth, but to them it can be a friendly greeting!

Alpha male mandrills have the brightest-colored markings. If they lose their power in the troop, their colors fade.

MANDRILL
FACT FILE

CLASS
MAMMAL

GROUP NAME
TROOP

TERRITORY
WEST AFRICAN RAINFOREST

HOW BIG!

AVERAGE LIFE SPAN
20 YEARS

DIET
OMNIVORE
FRUIT, SEEDS, NUTS, LEAVES, INSECTS

Did you know...

Mandrills have special pouches in their cheeks where they can save food for later.

MONKEY BUSINESS

People often get confused between monkeys and apes, but there is a very easy way to tell them apart: monkeys have tails and apes don't! Most monkeys have long tails, but mandrills and some other monkeys only have short, stubby tails.

85

How to draw... a mandrill

1. SHAGGY HEAD: Start by drawing a scruffy, furry head shape.

2. BACK AND TAIL: Draw a curved line for the back, and then a big, droopy tail.

3. BOTTOM AND LEG: Male mandrills are known for their big, colorful bottoms, so draw a circle underneath the tail for its bottom! Then add the back leg.

4. REST OF THE BODY: Copy the drawing below to create the other leg and arms.

5. FACE: Follow these three mini steps to create the face.

1. Face shape.

2. Add the nose and mouth area.

3. Then add the eyes, mouth and ears.

6. COLOR! Don't forget that famous bright red and blue face!

TURTLE

THIS AQUATIC REPTILE IS TURTLE-Y AWESOME!

Turtles are instantly recognizable by their big, tough shells. The shell acts like a shield to keep their soft bodies safe from predators! Some turtles have evolved to live almost their entire lives in the ocean, so we call them sea turtles. Their legs are shaped like flippers, which makes them powerful swimmers. The only time sea turtles come onto land is when the females lay their eggs. They return to the same beach every year to bury the eggs in the sand. When the baby turtles hatch, they have to scurry across the sand and into the sea. It's one of the most dangerous journeys they will ever make, because hungry birds and crabs try to catch them before they reach the water.

Fun Fact
The character of Crush in the Pixar film *Finding Nemo* is a Pacific green sea turtle.

Did you know...
If a turtle egg is buried in colder sand, the baby will be male, while eggs buried in warmer sand will be female.

Some turtles have soft, leathery shells instead of hard, bony ones.

GREEN TURTLE

FACT FILE

CLASS
REPTILE

GROUP NAME
BALE

TERRITORY
OCEANS AROUND THE WORLD

HOW BIG!

AVERAGE LIFE SPAN
70—80 YEARS

DIET
HERBIVORE
SEA GRASSES AND ALGAE

CONSERVATION STATUS
ENDANGERED

A turtle's shell is actually part of its skeleton! It is made of more than 50 bones.

Did you know...

Sea turtles migrate to find food or warmer waters, or to breed. Some can travel more than 10,000 miles!

TORTOISE OR TURTLE

With their famous shells, turtles and tortoises look very similar, but what's the difference? It can be a bit confusing because all tortoises are actually a type of turtle! Tortoises are what we call the turtles that live on land and can't swim.

How to draw... a turtle

1. SHELL: Draw an eye-shaped oval.

2. SHELL RIM: Add a rim to the bottom.

3. HEAD: Draw a little neck with a big head.

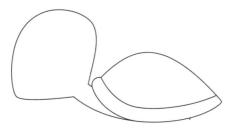

4. FLIPPERS: Draw four flipper shapes underneath the shell.

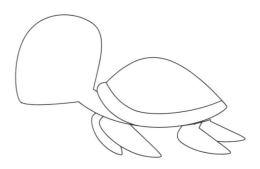

5. FACE: To make this baby turtle super cute, draw a really big eye, some oval-shaped markings on its head, and a lovely smile.

6. COLOR! Perhaps add some colorful coral around your baby turtle!

90

FLAMINGO

THESE MAGNIFICENT BIRDS ARE PINK DUE TO THEIR DIET

Birds are some of the animal kingdom's most colorful creatures, and few are as striking as the flamingo. These long-legged wading birds get their incredible pink feathers from the food they eat. The algae and shrimp that flamingos eat contain a red chemical, which gets absorbed into their bodies. The chemical ends up in their skin and feathers, gradually turning them pink. Flamingos don't have much competition for living space or food because they are one of the few creatures that can live in alkaline lakes. The water there would burn the skin off a human's legs! But thankfully, flamingos' scaly legs can cope with the conditions. They are beautiful, tough, and incredibly unique birds.

© Getty / Daniel Janess.Lowe

© Getty / Jaki good photography

Did you know...

Flamingo chicks start out white, but gain their pink color as they grow and eat.

A flamingo's diet is made up of crustaceans, plankton, and algae—all found in shallow waters.

Fun Fact

Flamingos get their name from the Spanish word flamenco which comes from the Latin word for fire!

GREATER FLAMINGO
FACT FILE

CLASS
BIRD

GROUP NAME
FLAMBOYANCE

TERRITORY
WETLANDS AND COASTS OF AFRICA, EUROPE & ASIA

HOW BIG!

AVERAGE LIFE SPAN
30—40 YEARS

DIET
OMNIVORE
ALGAE, SHRIMP, AND OTHER CRUSTACEANS

Flamingos can often be seen standing on one leg. This saves energy because it actually takes them more effort to stand on both legs!

Did you know...

Flamingos have curved beaks to help them scoop up their food from the water and mud.

STRENGTH IN NUMBERS

Flamingos live together in huge groups called colonies. They can include thousands of flamingos, although the biggest colony had more than one million! That makes life safer for the flamingos, because predators are less likely to attack a big group.

1. BODY: Start with an eye-shaped blob for the body.

2. LONG NECK: At the front of the body, draw a long, curved neck and the head.

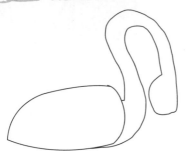

3. BEAK AND WING: Over the top of the body, draw the wing feathers. Then draw the beak—it should be a bit bent!

Erase the body line where the feathers now are.

Erase the original line that separated the body and neck.

4. TAIL AND LEG: Using an eraser and your pencil, turn the rear end of the body into tail feathers. Then draw the first leg.

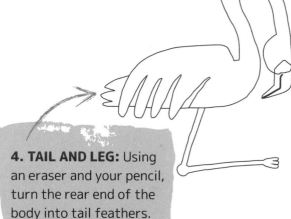

5. EYES AND STANDING LEG: Add two little eyes and eyebrows. Then draw the other leg straight down behind the bent leg.

Erase the line across the beak.

6. COLOR! Pink, purple. . . and more pink!

LEMUR

MEET MADAGASCAR'S UNIQUE PRIMATES

Lemurs are monkey-like animals that can only be found on Madagascar and some of the nearby islands. Scientists believe that lemurs' ancestors reached the African island on floating logs, branches, or other bundles of plants—like natural rafts! Because they existed away from other primates like monkeys and apes, they developed different abilities. There are more than 100 species of lemur, and most are nocturnal. They live most of their lives in trees, but some appear during the day to forage for food. When two males fight, they battle it out to make the stinkiest smell—whoever runs away first loses! Weirdly, this is also how they attract a mate.

©Getty / Luca Nichetti / EyeEm

Fun Fact

Lemurs have wet noses like dogs and cats. This gives them a really good sense of smell!

©iStock / Getty / Anolis01

Did you know...

Humans and blue-eyed black lemurs are some of the only primates to have blue eyes.

A lemur's big eyes help it to see better at night—and look super cute!

Unlike most other lemurs, ring-tailed lemurs are active during the day, and spend a lot of time on the ground.

RING-TAILED LEMUR
FACT FILE

CLASS
MAMMAL

GROUP NAME
TROOP

TERRITORY
MADAGASCAN FOREST

HOW SMALL!

AVERAGE LIFE SPAN
15—18 YEARS

DIET
HERBIVORE
FRUIT, LEAVES, BARK

CONSERVATION STATUS
ENDANGERED

Did you know...

? Male lemurs have scent glands on their wrists. They rub their wrists against trees to mark their territory.

TROOP LEADERS

Female lemurs are the center of their social group. They are the dominant ones who can push males away to get the best food and sleeping sites, and decide where the troop travels. This is unusual, as most other primate groups are led by the males.

How to draw...   a lemur

1. LITTLE HEAD: Start by drawing a cat-like head. Then add a chest panel, and a curved line for the back.

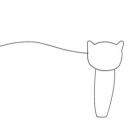

2. LOOPY LOOP: Draw an enormous curled tail. Then add the first arm.

3. MORE LEGS: From the other side of the chest, add the other arm. Then draw the tummy and a leg at the back.

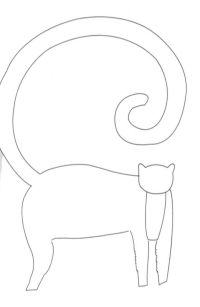

4. BACK LEG AND FEET: Underneath the tummy, draw a line from the front arm to the back leg. Draw the second leg here too. Then add all the hands and feet.

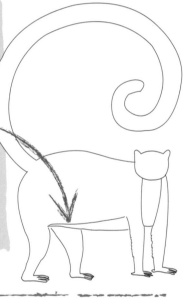

5. FACE: Draw two big eyes. Then add a little snout with a tiny nose and mouth.

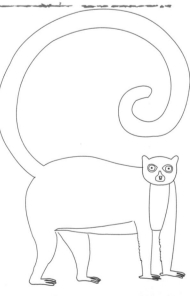

6. COLOR! Using black, add lots of stripes to the tail. Make those big eyes nice and bright with yellow.

SHARK

WHY THESE OCEAN PREDATORS AREN'T AS FEARSOME AS THEY SEEM

With their tiny, black eyes, large, powerful bodies, and rows of razor-sharp teeth, sharks definitely look like one of the scariest creatures in the world. However, you really shouldn't be scared of swimming in the sea, as it's incredibly rare for a shark to attack a human. In fact, people are more likely to get struck by lightning than attacked by a shark! Most sharks are carnivores and will eat fish, crustaceans, and molluscs. A few sharks are actually omnivores and will also eat sea grasses. Sharks don't eat much, usually less than 10% of their body weight per week. They spend most of their time conserving energy while lazily drifting around the ocean. See, not that scary after all!

©Getty / ullsteinbild

©Getty / VWPics

?Did you know...
The whale shark is the biggest shark in the world, but it mostly eats fish and plankton!

Some species of shark have to keep swimming, otherwise they wouldn't be able to breathe.

Most sharks are cold-blooded to survive in cold water, but great white sharks are partially warm-blooded.

GREAT WHITE SHARK
FACT FILE

– – – – – – –

CLASS
CARTILAGINOUS FISH

GROUP NAME
SHIVER

TERRITORY
OCEANS WORLDWIDE

AVERAGE LIFE SPAN
60 YEARS

DIET
CARNIVORE
OTHER FISH AND
MARINE MAMMALS,
LIKE SEALS

HOW BIG!

Fun Fact
Sharks have teeth stacked up inside their mouths to replace any that fall out!

Did you know...
Some sharks are very speedy swimmers. The shortfin mako shark can reach speeds of over 34 mph!

NATURAL BORN HUNTERS
Sharks are some of the most effective predators in the world. They are able to see in the dark really well, have a fantastic sense of smell, and have powerful jaws with hundreds of razor-sharp teeth. Sharks can also sense electrical signals produced by their prey!

How to draw... a shark

1. BACK AND FINS: Draw a large, backwards "C" shape. Add a big, pointy fin, and a smaller one just below it.

2. TAIL: At the bottom of the arch, add the tail like this.

3. NOSE: At the top, add the head with a little bump for the nose.

4. FIN AND GILLS: Draw a curved line from the tail up towards the nose, but not quite joining up with the nose. Add a small fin and gill lines on the body.

Erase the lines across the fins.

5. TUMMY AND TEETH: Add a line from the nose, through the gill lines to the tail. Then draw the mouth and add lots of teeth!

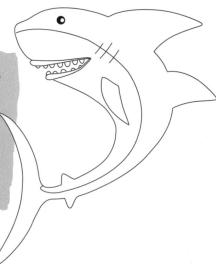

6. COLOR! Why not draw some extra underwater friends for your shark to play with?

EAGLE

THIS SHARP-EYED BIRD IS LOOKING GREAT!

Eagles are some of the most instantly recognizable birds in the world. They are known for their amazing eyesight, which is why we use the phrase "eagle-eyed" for people with good vision. An eagle can spot its prey from up to three miles away! It then dives at speeds of up to 150 miles per hour to grab its dinner in its powerful claws. Eagles usually hunt for fish and small mammals like rabbits, but some species also eat reptiles and other birds. Eagles live on every continent except Antarctica, but most species live in Europe. An eagle usually builds its nests high up in trees or on cliff edges, where it can keep an eye out for prey below.

©Getty / Daniel Hernanz Ramos

Fun Fact

Because it hunts for its own food, the eagle is known as a bird of prey.

? Did you know...

Eagles can see both forward and to the side from each eye at the same time, giving them incredible vision.

BALD EAGLE

FACT FILE

- - - - - - -

CLASS
BIRD

GROUP NAME
CONVOCATION

TERRITORY
WORLDWIDE

AVERAGE LIFE SPAN
20—30 YEARS

DIET
CARNIVORE
FISH AND
SMALL MAMMALS

Eagles have incredibly powerful feet with super sharp talons. Some species can crush the skulls of their prey!

HOW BIG!

? Did you know...
Once an eagle finds a mate, they usually stay together for life. Both parents help to raise their young.

ICONIC BIRDS

Eagles are popular choices as national birds. The bald eagle is a famous symbol of the USA; the golden eagle is the national bird of Mexico and Scotland; Namibia, Zambia, Zimbabwe, and South Sudan are represented by the African fish eagle.

How to draw... an eagle

1. HEAD: Start by drawing this shape—it's like half of a cracked eggshell!

2. GHOSTLY BODY: Draw the body with a shape like this, a bit like a ghost.

3. LEGS: From the little bumps at the bottom of the body, add two bird feet.

4. WING: Add a nice big wing on top of the body shape.

Erase the parts of the face that cut through the beak.

5. FACE: Draw a curved beak and a large eye.

6. COLOR! When you're coloring your eagle, add some wiggly lines to create feathers on the wing. Why not also add a branch for your eagle to perch on?

FOX

HOW FANTASTIC IS THE FOX?

Foxes are close relatives of dogs and wolves, sharing the same bushy tail, furry coat, black nose, and pointy ears. They are powerful predators and usually hunt small mammals and birds, like rabbits and chickens. But foxes are actually omnivores, so they'll sometimes eat grasses, fruit, and flowers. They are also scavengers, which means they will eat prey that has been killed by other predators like bears or wolves. Foxes are famous for being cunning creatures, but what makes them so successful is their ability to adapt to changes. They have successfully changed their diet, habitat, and sleeping pattern to cope with the impact humans have had on their environment.

©Getty / Justin Lo

Did you know...
For camouflage, Arctic foxes grow a white coat in winter, but shed it when the snow melts so they turn brown or gray.

Fun Fact
Foxes can make about 20 different noises when communicating with each other!

©Getty / Reinhard Holzl

Did you know...
Foxes raise their young in underground dens. They also use the den as a place to store extra food.

A fox's ears can rotate to help it locate its prey.

RED FOX
FACT FILE

CLASS
MAMMAL

GROUP NAME
SKULK

TERRITORY
GLOBAL

HOW BIG!

AVERAGE LIFE SPAN
2—5 YEARS

DIET
OMNIVORE
SMALL ANIMALS, FRUIT, GRASSES

The red fox can survive in lots of different environments, from forests and cities to deserts and mountains!

URBAN JUNGLE

Foxes are remarkable because they are so adaptable and resourceful. Some have learned to live alongside humans, and have made their homes in towns and cities. Up to half of an urban fox's diet is made up of stuff stolen out of our trash cans!

How to draw... a fox

1. BODY: Draw a cone-like shape like this, with two pointy ears at the top.

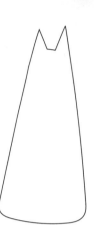

2. SNOUT: From the left ear, draw a nose shape like this, and then erase the original line.

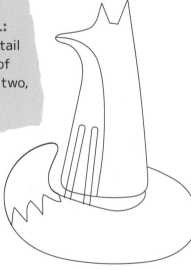

3. TUMMY: Starting from the center of the nose, draw a curved line down.

4. LEGS AND TAIL: Draw a big, bushy tail around the front of the body, and add two, thin front legs.

5. FACE: Draw a small triangle inside each ear. Then add an oval nose, a small mouth, and a big eye like this.

Erase the parts of the body line that cut through the legs.

6. COLOR! We have gone for a lovely orange for our fox. If you wanted to, you could make yours an Arctic fox and keep the fur white.

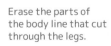